Moments

In

Time

J Wilkinson

Editing by: Lisa Borne Graves

Cover and Interior Design by: Jessica Tilles/TWA Solutions

ISBN: 9798986900209

I dedicate this book to LR *Wilkinson,*
for it is through her that I have learned what true love
really is and what it means to be absolutely cared for.

CONTENTS

When I turned and
faced grief
I saw that it was just
love
staring back at me

How do we save these

Moments in Time

This heart

This heart has been broken this heart
has been used
This heart feels loss this heart
misses you
This heart has its locks this heart
has its cell
This heart is filled with grief
This heart has been through hell
This heart cried endlessly this heart
stayed true
This heart still knows love this heart still
loves you

Chapter One

YOU HAVE A VOICE

This book has a purpose: it's to give me a voice and you a voice. It's going to remind you, even teach you, to stop and notice, or perhaps remember, those "moments in time." Those little times like a ride in the car or sharing secrets on the phone, ordinary moments that can easily slip by unnoticed, but believe me, if you no longer have that person here with you, those little moments will mean the world to you.

Through words and illustrations, I hope to share my feelings, feelings of love, but also sadness. Feelings that are sometimes just rolled up and neatly titled Grief. Don't for one minute ever let anyone confuse you about grief. It is pure love. Love that simply has no way to express itself.

Normally when you love someone and you feel that need to share it, you go up to them and you say it, "I love you" or you express it, by hugging them but with grief, you are left with these ever-challenging feelings and needs and having nowhere to take them can become overwhelming.

You find yourself missing this person and needing them. Everyday things will remind you of them and all the experiences you shared and although you don't want those memories to stop, you know deep inside you have to find a way to deal with them and not just burst out crying each time.

Whether it's a close friend, spouse, partner, parent, child, your beloved pet, or other relative, the death of a loved one can feel overwhelming. You may experience waves of intense and very difficult emotions, ranging from complete sadness, emptiness, and despair, to shock, numbness, guilt, or regret. You might rage at the circumstances of your loved one's death—your anger focused on yourself, doctors, other loved ones, or God. You may even find it difficult to accept that your person or pet is really gone, or struggle to see how you can ever recover and move on from your loss.

What is *moving on?*

Even saying that upsets me.

As if we are just going to wake up one day, and it's all over. We just "moved on." What a stupid way of saying it. Of course, what is trying to be said with that statement is that we are learning to live and go forward with our lives without this loved one being physically with us.

The real challenge is how do we?

The first step is we learn to accept and believe they are still with us, inside us, right there in our hearts and minds. How do we learn to trust that and embrace that? How do we find enough comfort in that to move forward with our lives and in doing so, take them with us?

Believe me, those little moments in time will come racing back into your memory and before you say you don't want that, STOP and think again. Because you will. You will find yourself completely surviving by those memories. Before you know it, everywhere you go you will hear something said or see something that just triggers a memory of your loved one and you will be so thankful for it, as if they sent a personal message just to you. You may start to cry just like I am right now writing this, but it's a mixture of sad and happy tears, tears and memories you wouldn't give up for anything in the world.

Those "Moments in Time" are our lifeline to that loved one. I'm telling you, no, I'm begging you, to embrace them with everything inside of you. They are how we will survive this; they are the answer to recovering from total despair to finding a way to continue to live.

There is no doubt that the level of support you have around you, your personality, and your own levels of health and well-being can all play a role in how grief impacts you following a loss. But no matter how much pain you're in right now, it's important to know that there are healthy ways to cope with these emotions and come to terms with your grief.

While life may never be quite the same again—let me resay that… Your life, my life, *will* never be the same again—but in time, we can ease our sorrow, start to look to the future with hope and optimism, and eventually move forward with our lives.

Whatever your relationship was to the loved one or pet who died, it's important to remember that we all grieve in different ways. There's no single way to react. When you lose someone important in your life, it's okay to feel how you feel. Some people express their pain by crying, others never shed a tear—but that doesn't mean they feel the loss any less.

Don't judge yourself or think that you should behave in a different way or try to impose a timetable on your grief. Grieving a death takes time. For some people, that time is measured in weeks or months. For others, it's in years. In many ways, it will be a lifetime.

You absolutely must allow yourself the opportunity and time to feel and process the grief and go through parts of the mourning process, even though this can trigger many intense and unexpected emotions. But the pain of your grief won't go away faster if you ignore it. In fact, trying to do so may only make things worse in the long run. To eventually find a way to come to terms with your loss, you'll need to actively face the pain.

It's been said the only cure for grief is to grieve.

WHEN DOES IT END

*When does the pain stop when does
it end
will I wake up and this sorrow will
end
perhaps this is a life sentence each
day
I live over and over again
the memories are my lifeline
as I search through them
from the very beginning
to what is thought of as the end
as if I let one slip away I would
be losing you all over again
then darkness comes calling and I
lay down to put this day to end
knowing in the morning
it just starts all over again*

Chapter Two

YOU NEED TO BE AWARE...

You need to be aware and prepared. Some days the pain of your grief may seem more manageable than others. Then a reminder such as a photo, a piece of music, or a simple memory can trigger a wave of painful emotions again. While you can't always plan for such reminders, you can be prepared for an upcoming holiday, anniversary, or birthday that may reignite your grief. Talk to other friends and family ahead of time and agree on the best ways to mark such occasions. But never just pretend it's not real or that it didn't happen.

Moving on doesn't mean forgetting your loved one.

Finding a way to continue forward with your life doesn't mean your pain will end or your loved one will be forgotten. Most of us carry our losses with us throughout life; they become part of who we are. The pain should gradually become easier to bear, but the memories and the love you had for them will always remain.

6

Let me warn some of you who are pretending this loss didn't happen or you're not going to deal with it. This lack of action will only make it grow larger and manifest in other ways and areas in your life, whether it be health, relationships, and/or mentally. You're not going to just stick your head in the sand and move along; you will deal with it whether you like it or not.

Take it from me, take it from the many people I have talked with. You can't avoid ever facing it. Now you will be able to keep yourself busy and your thoughts on other things but at some point, grief will corner you and absolutely force you to acknowledge your pain and feelings. My suggestion, my plea to you, is that you just face it head on to the best of your ability and ask for help all along the way. Trust me, even though this will hurt, it's still better than running away.

This is a club that no one wants to be in; the membership came at the highest of possible prices. You will always be a member just as I will, and you will always be dealing with this loss and empty feeling. So, with that amount of leverage stacked against us, shouldn't we accept our position and dare ourselves to be a survivor of this enormous challenge?

fully Exposed

you may think you're safe, you're
invulnerable
that you are somehow protected
but one day
something is going to come along
that will shake loose the scar tissue
and when it falls away and you are
standing there fully exposed
it's going to rip you to the core
and it's going to hurt like HELL....

I've learned to miss you quietly
More than you'll ever know

If only the voices in my head knew that...

Chapter Three

EMOTIONS

When you lose someone you love, it's normal
to want to cut yourself off from others, to run
and hide in your shell. But this just isn't the right
time to be alone. Even when you don't feel able to
talk about your loss, simply being around other
people who care about you can provide comfort
and help ease the pain from the grief.
Reaching out to those who care about you can
also be an important first step on the road to
healing. While some friends and relatives
may be uncomfortable with your grief, plenty
of others will be eager to lend support. Talking
about your thoughts and feelings won't make
you a burden. You will hear this little voice telling
you, *no one cares, no one wants to hear it,*
keep it to yourself, but don't give in to that voice. That
road leads you nowhere. Instead, be strong, find
that friend or neighbor who listens and reassures
you with care who will do even more.

I suggest you write your feelings out, maybe in a journal
or just write it down to give yourself permission to
say what you need and it's okay to be mad and to
say hard heartfelt things. Don't let anyone
convince you that you shouldn't.
You have your feelings, and I have mine. They
don't have to be the same, and you get to express
yours just like I do, so writing them out just may be
the help you need.
This can also help you make sense of your loved
one's death and find ways to honor their memory.

Lean on friends and family.

Even those closest to you can struggle to know
how to help during a time of loss like this, so do
not hesitate to tell others what you need—whether
it's helping with funeral arrangements or just
being around to talk. If you don't feel you have
anyone you can lean on for support at this
difficult time, look to local churches and grief
organizations, widen your social network. That
sounds crazy when you are at your lowest, to try
and go out and make new friends, but you need
help. You need a lifeline, and when someone
is drowning, they do anything it takes to survive.
I want you to realize you are up to your throat
in water, and you will stand there and drown
unless you decide to fight for survival.

THIS PAIN

that pain your carrying around
on the inside of you
it's slowly killing you
you want to get better
but you simply must realize
you're the only one
that can control it and let it go
you want to get better
but how do you
you want to get better
but each day feels the same
you want to get better
but somehow, you must admit
you feel them more in the
pain......

EVERYTHING IS DIFFERENT

THINGS WILL NEVER BE THE SAME
DON'T EVER EXPECT THEM TO BE

Chapter Four

LONELY HURTS

I'm in pieces

I'm standing here in pieces
Realizing I've gotta find
A way to escape
The life I had made is suddenly changed
Never ever to be the same
GOD has the control in this I know
I'm aware he will never let me go

But I'm standing here in pieces
Realizing I gotta find
A way to escape
Time is my friend is all
The crowd screams
Over and over again

I get it, I get it
But when
Does my
Sentencing end

Celebrate your loved one...

Of course, we should celebrate our loved one's life. Funeral or memorial service can fulfill important functions, allowing you to acknowledge, celebrate their life and all they mean to you, and reflect on the passing. Remember their life, and taking the time needed to say goodbye is so important.

In the period after a funeral, however, your grief can often become even more intense. Often, other people may appear to have moved on, while you're left struggling to make sense of your "new normal." It's very difficult to see others simply going on with life as if nothing ever happened, but you don't know what they're feeling on the inside or if they have somehow suppressed the pain and just don't realize it's going to have to be dealt with at some point. Don't spend your time and energy worrying about how others seem to care or don't care; we all are different, and you are just in charge of yourself.

Remembering your loved one does not have to end with the funeral though. Finding ways of celebrating the loved one can help maintain their memory and provide comfort as you move through the grieving process.

*Pictures, items of theirs, things that
bring back happy memories
are great to have around.*

I wear a bracelet, a simple leather bracelet I was
given that has a small picture of my son and I
together, and it helps remind me that I have
him with me always. It's just a simple
bracelet that reminds me of a very happy
"moment in time" that we shared, a moment I
wouldn't take anything for and a memory that
I will carry with me for the rest of my life.
But still I woke up early one morning and wrote this.

Maybe if I hide my
sadness,
you want see it and neither
will I

This unhappiness inside

I'm tired of feeling this unhappiness
inside me

I know this is not the way you would
want me to be

I'm trying to adjust I'm trying to set
you completely free

But how do I do it and still carry you
always inside of me

I've almost never been without you that's
the difficulty

I search for you in my dreams hoping you
will come to me

Only to wake up feeling more lonely

I know this is not the answer
I know GOD wants more for me

I just keep pushing forward
knowing the future will one day

Reunite you and me

Chapter Five

MY WRITINGS

I can only blame

The depth of my love

For the depth

Of
My
wounds

MOVING FORWARD

*Sometimes in life
you must stand alone*

**It just doesn't seem right
you have this feeling inside
what your doing is wrong**

but

*Sometimes in life you
have to stand alone.*

My thoughts know me
not the me you see
the real me

Grief is like a terminal illness
In and out of remission
With a constant goal to choke
The very life out of you

I don't recognize me in the
mirror anymore
The emptiness the sadness
that hovers over me
Imprisoned for not a crime
that I did but
was laid upon me
Sentenced and shackled against
my very will
Forever to carry the burden and
marks of mental anguish
But if this is my only way
to feel
Then cuff and chain me
for eternity

Why…

Don't ask why the crowd cried
But how am I not to wonder why
This is going to challenge me
for a lifetime
Some say it's just a mystery
Gods plan you see
So where does this plan leave me
I'm not being rebellious you see
Just asking the many questions that
Seem to haunt me…

SHARE YOUR PAIN

They say sharing your pain makes it hurt
a little less
Then I suggest you make the world listen
really fast
Scream it to the crowd as they race past
Anything that makes the pain not last
Bring everyone in the circle if it makes
it pass
I'll stop screaming it as soon as the
feelings
of pain surpass

Here's my hand

There are times it feels the rain is
literally blowing in your face
It can even feel as if there is simply no
one there to embrace
In those times you feel you have
absolutely no place
But try to hold strong

The cold will blow and chill your bones
you will fall asleep and wake up alone
But try to hold on

Loneliness will scare you and grief will bite
you simply feel no reason to still fight
But try to hold strong

You're not the only one you're not
struggling all alone
here take my hand together we will
walk on

Meet grace

today I was reintroduced to grace
I found him to be all he's built up to be
I was surprised he wanted to spend
time with someone like me
today it was just God's grace and me

why yes, you're welcome to ride to
work with me
honestly, I just want to thank you for
remembering me
I'm sorry I've not reached out to you
I've been really busy you see
yes, I've allowed the things of this
world to completely consume me
this is nice just God's grace and me

I want to thank you for spending this
simple day with just me

What's that...

You have a message for me
God Himself is that concerned for me
I sometimes forget all He's done for
me you see

I will take time to remember
I've just been so busy being me...

I hear you calling I know
it's you
I hear you calling but really
 what do you want me to do
The truth is sometimes I hear you
 I just don't want to listen to you
I'm obviously in this fog and I realize
 I got to make it through
The devil is sitting on the edge of the bed,
and he often pretends to be you
I hear you calling I know it's you
I'm sorry God for these terrible feelings
but you know they're true
What am I going to do try and hide
 my thoughts and feelings from you
I hear you calling there's no way
 I would ever leave you
I hear you calling GOD
Deep down I know you're going to
pull me through

Mad at you

So did you really think leaving me here all alone was
the right thing to do
Did you even consider your family your love ones how
we would miss you
I mean you had to realize just how much our world
revolves around you
Did you think about your friends how they would be lost
without you
What about the fact that it's always been me and you
 it's always been us two
I don't know a me without you
I mean really did you think this through
Was this somehow in the plans ever since the first day
God gave me you
That would be very hard to accept as the truth
I guess you can tell I woke up a little mad at you....
Deep down I know I have no choice but to get over this
and of course to forgive you
I look forward to the day I'm back together with you
I guess you can tell I woke up a little mad at you

The cloud of grief
It follows you to bed at night
and meets you in the car each morning

The cloud of grief
It savagely creeps up your body until it grips your throat
squeezes the very breath out of you

The cloud of grief
Determined to suck any joy that could be in your day
and if by some chance joy slips in through a crack.
Grief is right there to make sure you feel guilty for it

The cloud of grief
tells you the suns not that bright
the sky's not that blue

Grief I don't belong to you
shake you off, that's what I will do
I have to make my mind to stand up against you
you're not going to control my every move
No Grief I don't belong to you

I hear you whispering

There are times when I feel I can't see this through

I hear you whispering devil I know it's not true

You are toying with my emotions as if I would ever listen to you

You offer dark remedies things I would never do

You're wasting your breath devil I know that it's you

Not loneliness again please try something new

Fine I will lay here in bed and wait it through

Oh, devil you have so much to say but you must take

me for a fool

You've nothing to offer and this journey

I will travel without you

The world just keeps going on as my friends
 ask why I stay home

you need to get out they say it's not good to
 be alone

Oh, I'm not alone
My boy's not here but he's not gone

Come go to the ball game there's so many
 things we can do
You got to let him go it's not good for you

Good for me? They don't have a clue
Like I'm somehow capable of living life
 without you

Oh, I'm not alone

My boy is not here but he's not gone

One thing I'm being taught, the true definition of lonely

Oh, but I'm not alone

My boy is not here but he will never be gone

I SCREAMED OUT

And I screamed out
How could you God?
Why would you?

God said nothing..

I screamed out
Where were you God?
Why didn't you?

God said nothing..

I screamed out
How dare you God
How could you?

God whispered
How dare I ?
Where was I ?
How could I ?
Do you honestly think you're better off than he is?
Do you think for one single moment he would be better there,
than here?

Where was I?

I was there when you first saw him

I was there when he began to walk

I was there when he told you he was sick

I was there when he left to come here...

So, I ask you.

How dare YOU....

You think you know me

but

you don't know me

You don't know the real me
You don't know the scared me
You don't know the lonely me
You don't know the needy me

you think you know me, but you don't know me

You don't know the me that's trapped in memories

the way I close those doors because I don't want to think
You don't know the lonely me

the way I somehow find comfort in being lonely
You don't know the needy me

what a hunger this need inside of me

You think you know me, but you don't know me

You only know the me that you see as me

Tell me your story I'll tell you mine

Tell me your story I'll tell you mine
I'll share in your story and then you can share
in mine
No matter what your need I'll give you my time
Tell me about your love allow me to tell you
about mine
The comfort of others can be so hard to find
I'll take it from strangers if they'll just except
mine
We open our hearts something we never
planned
All In the hopes that somehow together will be
able to understand
God has our hearts God has a plan
I'll share in your story and then you can share
in mine
Tell me your story I'll tell you mine

I
Feel
You
Day
And
Night

You can't just ignore grief and hope to power through. You will have to allow yourself to process the grief and start the healing journey.

I write
words to
keep from
 crying

I'm different
than before

Things will never be the same anymore

I miss the old me

It's important to remember anger, bitterness, resentment are all normal feelings after a loss.

You might have anxiety; dread and you definitely will be consumed with sadness as your forced to come to terms with these feelings and the loss that you're going through.

It's okay to cry or admit that you're angry or frustrated. Don't keep those emotions pent up inside you allowing them to turn into resentment and depression.

Sometimes facing it is the only way through.

I lay down at night

And I think

About you

If you want to walk right into my dreams

Don't let me stand in the way

BECAUSE I'M LOOKING FOR YOU TO....

I realize I can never bring you back

But with my pen

I can see that they never

Forget about you…

words

can

paint

a

picture

that

allows

you

to

see

inside

of

me

and they call that poetry

Chapter Six

GRIEF IS LOVE

Grief is the price we pay for an amazing and great love.

Grief is all that love you want to give but just feel that you can't. It is love that you simply have no knowledge of a way to give, so it leaves you frustrated and lost in what to do. That feeling can paralyze you in your tracks. Let's face it, no one has ever taught us what to do in this situation and unfortunately, there is no one-size-fits-all solution.

Love is a tremendous force in our lives. We all know the feelings of meeting someone and being completely overwhelmed with their presence and feeling the "butterflies" that often consume our ability to think and use good judgment. Well, that same love is running wild inside our minds and thoughts although it may quiet down and lay dormant at times. When we experience the loss of someone, it comes roaring back to the surface and demands to be a managing force in your life and in your feelings.

When love is lost, we feel as though we lose the part of us that did the loving. We honestly feel the hole and the emptiness.

I promise when grief comes it's nothing like you expect it to be, depending on the magnitude of your love it can feel as though.

Your complete purpose to live is being separated from your very soul.

I wake up each morning I lay there missing you

This is definitely the longest I've ever been without you

I get up I get dressed I head to work knowing I won't see you

Don't get me wrong my life is good it's just completely different now without you

THE CROWD

The crowd says I'm going to be OK I'll get through

But this is definitely the longest I've ever been without you

The hardest part is knowing really nothing I can do

But this is definitely the longest I've ever been without you

I lay down at night and I realize the crowd was right that's another day I just got through

But this is definitely the longest I've ever been without you

Don't spend time asking "what if".

That's a question we could be asking forever

and never get a real answer. Closure will only

start once we accept our situation and start

to push forward.

I'm fine really

What's that

how I'm doing

I'm doing just fine

except I don't sleep, and I just lay there till dawn

No, I don't go out much I just enjoy being alone

I haven't been talking to them really, I just don't answer my phone

No, I think I'll just stay here I really like it at home

but really as you can see

how am I doing

I'm doing just fine...

There will come a time when you really have no choice but to accept what has happened.

Slowly you will wrap your mind around reality and at that point, you will start to look back and realize all that you had and all the important things you're going to miss.

It is so very hard to accept, but then you can start to heal and be thankful for the Moments in Time that you had together.

I wish we laughed like before

I need it now so much more

I just wish we could laugh like before

I don't know about yours
But
I know about mine
My
Broken heart needs repair

Chapter Seven

FIVE STAGES OF GRIEF

- Denial

- Anger

- Bargaining

- Depression

- Acceptance

Grief isn't over days after our loved one dies.
It's just the beginning of a life-long journey.

5 stages of grief
denial
anger
bargaining
depression
acceptance

I'm sure you have heard of these five stages of grief or at least some version of them.

All of these are very likely to surface in your life and thoughts.

The truth is it can be much easier if you are aware and not alarmed or frightened by each emotion.

Denial

Denial is the first thing that takes hold of us, and it often sounds like this:

This just can't be true; I don't believe this really happened or *I'm never going to accept this is real.*

Unfortunately, or perhaps fortunately, denial stops the brain from thinking fully and rationally, and its purpose is to protect us from information we simply can't register at that time. But it doesn't stop the fact that we are going to have to at some point.

A small amount of denial may seem to linger forever, because it may just be that you have nowhere in your thinking process to truly allow this to be a fact, and that's okay as long as you realize deep down that reality can't be changed and time can't be turned back.

Anger

Anger is a completely natural emotion after your loved one dies. Their death can seem completely cruel and unfair to you, especially when you feel they have died before their time, or you begin to think about all the plans you had for the future together.

It's also common to feel anger towards the one who has died, thoughts like how they could leave you, and why they didn't do more to stop this.

You can easily experience anger at yourself for things you did or didn't do before their death. Don't let this consume you.

Bargaining

Bargaining can happen when we are in pain, and it's sometimes hard to accept that there's nothing we can do to change things. We can very easily start to make deals with ourselves, or perhaps with God, as if we somehow think we have any control, but that's just it. The fact that we must face that we have absolutely zero control is what leads us to the irrational thought to bargain. We just want and need to believe that if we act in particular ways, we will feel better.

It's also very common to find ourselves going over and over things that happened in the past and asking a lot of 'what if' questions, just wishing we could go back in time and change things. All of this is in the hope things could have turned out differently.

Depression

This feeling can come over you in waves. Strong intense feelings of pain and sadness. Life can simply feel like it has no purpose, no meaning, and this can be extremely scary and overwhelming. Avoid isolating yourself from others. Don't allow yourself to stay locked up inside and avoid people.

You absolutely must push through this. Remember, you will make it.

You will recover.

Acceptance

Acceptance is a terribly slow mover for most of us. Grief is still coming like waves, and pain is right there reminding us, moment by moment, of our loss. But ever so gradually, we will start to feel the pain easing and start to possibly accept what has happened.

The truth is you may never get over the death of your loved one, but you can learn to accept it. Slowly, you can start to be okay with living, knowing that you are holding and keeping their memories and moments close to your heart.

Chapter Eight

DON'T HOLD IT INSIDE

Don't think for even a minute that it's a good idea to try and hold this pain inside. Some people try to suppress their feelings and just stuff it all down deep; that's never going to be healthy and never going to work for you.

I want to reshare with you the thought of starting journaling. It's a perfect way to just get your thoughts out and give you a way to express yourself without anyone judging you or giving back unwanted or unneeded opinions.

This is not to stop you from sharing with a friend or a family member but simply allowing you to just say any and everything that you feel and think without any need to filter. Take it from me, as someone who started this process long before I lost my son. It has always been helpful to relieve my mind, and I definitely went to it as a grieving method. There are just times when your thoughts are not proper enough to share with anyone, but they are still your thoughts and just writing them out and getting them out of your mind, your heart, your soul, can become a complete life saver.

You don't

need to

heal all alone

we all hurt together

Now, if this is a completely new concept to you, then I probably am starting to lose you, but please stay with me. You don't have to write a book or buy anything; you can start with just paper and a pencil. Give me one solid week of effort, and I can almost promise you you're going to find out that it has helped in so many ways. You will find yourself saying things that you haven't even allowed yourself to think, and you will be able to just say it and cry it out.

Sometimes, we men and women need to give ourselves the permission to just break down and let go. There's no shame in it.

If you like, you can download a simple app on your phone to write on or you can purchase a journaling book that can prompt you each day to help keep you on track and push you along, but the main thing is that you do it. This has been one of the best things that I use to relieve the pressure and built-up thoughts and feelings. I can't express enough how much I want you to try writing this during this grieving period and beyond.

Journaling helps short circuit the stress following traumatic events. Reconnecting and becoming more comfortable with suppressed memories calm the fear center of the brain, which is in overdrive during the grieving process.

Use this journaling to get in touch with thoughts, memories, and emotions buried deep within you. Sometimes, you may find that you're writing around a topic that you can't grasp; you just can't bring it up with anyone. It's so upsetting you can't quite put your finger on it. That's because these difficult memories are being suppressed. Writing and then reading it over helps you get to the root of it. Often, the most therapeutic benefit of journaling is returning over and over and reading those past previous entries. With each review, you will find yourself growing stronger and beginning to learn to comprehend those painful thoughts. Even though it doesn't seem possible, you will be able to face them. That's when you are finally able to grasp that this is real, and you must deal with it.

The more you learn to be completely honest with yourself, the more you push yourself to face it, face it all—the bad feelings and the good—the sooner you're going to look back and see the progress you've made.

And remember, progress doesn't mean you forget about them; it doesn't mean you "moved on."

It means you learn how to live without your loved one, with the fact that you can't see them, but you feel them; you can't hear their voice, but you hear them speak to you; you don't see them in front of you, but you take them everywhere you go.

Maybe they're not here, but they're not gone...

Never be ashamed

of the scars

from

your battles

to

survive...

I

Cry

For both the life you lived

And for the one

You didn't get....

One thing I've learned is no one gets through this life without loss. We all deal with death and loss at some point.

the crowd
 says
you have to recover
from grief

RECOVER ....

you don't recover from love
you hold on to it no matter
the pain...

as long as I breathe
I will miss you
as long as I miss you
I will hurt
as long as I hurt
I will love you

We all deal with grief differently, but we share certain things. Emotions, pain, sorrow, these are all common feelings that human beings share. Each one of us needs to express our thoughts and be with others. We all need to be heard and have a chance to share our emotions. I want to encourage you to reach out to someone and find ways to get these hurt feelings out.

I really miss you so much kevin
I really miss you so much ke
I really miss you so much
I really miss you so mu
I really miss you so
I really miss you
I really miss y
I really mis
I really
I really lov
I really love y
I really love you
I really love you so
I really love you so mu
I really love you so much
I really love you so much ke
I really love you so much kevin

Turning off my mind

Is easier than dealing

With what's

Inside of it...

Chapter Nine

THE REALITY OF GRIEF

The reality here is that grief changes you. After death, it tries to become your identity. Your emotions are now fully on high alert, making sure you have your guard up for anything else that's traumatic. It affects your daily relationships. You may think you're shoving it down and distracting yourself. But the truth is, it's coming out in other ways.

You're more irritable, more on edge, realize you haven't cried in two months, and then suddenly, you're crying in the shower or the car. You're ghosting your friends because you just can't talk about it yet. You're ignoring your family because you just can't always deal with it. There's a painful tinge of jealousy when someone says, "my sister and I did this," "I just got off the phone with my son," "I just love my pet," "I'm going to see my mom." Whatever the sentence is, whoever the loss is to you. There's that painful stab in your heart when you hear someone talking about something regarding their loved one, because you don't get to do that anymore. It was ripped away from you...

Grief is ugly, and it is raw. And grief does change who you are. Grief has many faces, yet somehow no one ever grieves the same. Grief is lonely. Grief is intense, and grief does affect your life.

Whether you want to admit it or not.
But you, (we) me, will get through it, and
it's really okay to not be okay.

Remember there is no timeline for when you will feel ready to take a step forward.

But you will need to move forward at some point. You are going to need to pull all the pieces together and push forward

Stop and listen

For in our silences

We hide the loudest of words...

If not careful

we will spend

all our time

worrying about things we can't even change

when we should

spend our free time

Just learning how to live...

I wake up I miss you

I reach for my pen because it's the weapon I use
I look around in this empty room I feel the sorrow I feel
the gloom

I reach for my pen because it's the weapon I use
I realize I can't bring you back no matter what I do
but with my pen I can see that they never forget about
you

I reach for my pen because it's the weapon I use
Forever you'll live through the words that I use
Forever I'll share of the memory of you
I wake up I miss you I reached for my pen because it's
the weapon I use
as I write I fight to honor you

Life don't work the way you want

doesn't mean you're doing it wrong

people hurt you and little parts of
your heart turn to stone

but that doesn't always mean you're
doing something wrong

You're just trying to get through life

you look to the right you look to the
left the crowd is already gone

making it through is just up

to you alone

Chapter Ten

GRIEF
IS NOT THE ENEMY

That pain you're carrying around

On the inside of you

It's slowly killing you

You want to get better

But you have to realize

That you're the only one

that can let it go

You want to get better

But how do you

You want to get better

But each day is the same

I want to get better

But somehow, I feel you more

in the pain...

IF

Is the price we pay for loving

then I will never stop PAYING

SOMETIMES
WE JUST
HAVE TO GO
THROUGH THINGS

don't try and deal with all this grief alone.

You need help.

GRIEF

to be so broken
to have fallen
so far

that

the only thing
left to do

is to

Get Up…

NO, GRIEF IS NOT MY ENEMY ...

Is it a curse to grieve?

I think not...

Grief is a symbol of love, pure love. The heart clings to grief as if it's a last refuge, a final act of defiance or final stand. As if grief thinks it's going to stop and completely refuse any and all moving on, but grief isn't the enemy, you know, in fact grief, isn't even sad it's not something to run from as if you're in a horror flick, there's nothing wrong with accepting grief as a temporary companion.

You see when you really look at grief for what it is, you realize grief is the acknowledgment of life.

The acknowledgment of a love, a life and a love that you cherish and don't ever want to forget.

When you think you want to forget grief knows better, and grief will remind you that hurting is better than forgetting. Be wary of people who just move on as if this was just a bump in the road or a wrinkle in time. Because yes, we all can grieve differently but where there's true love there will be grief. Grief is a promise to remember they were here, they are loved, and they left a hole in the hearts of all that knew them.

Grief is just proof that you will be a part of us forever in every moment of happiness, in every adventure, every dream, every prayer, and every act of kindness, in each breath we take.

When the wind blows, I will feel you, in every turn of time I will remember you, I will carry you with me until they bury me and we can touch in person again. Every time I look into the mirror I will see you, when I take my last breath, I will reach for you.

NO, GRIEF IS NOT MY ENEMY...

It is a banner that our love was real, and I'll gladly hold that banner high...

Sleeping

Is

Just

A reset

For

A better

Day

Tomorrow...

They say death

Is forever

I say

Love is for

Eternity

The thing about grief that no one wants to talk about, is how lonely it feels. Even when you're in a crowded room and everyone there loves you and supports you. But you, yourself, are in this bubble of emptiness.

I say a bubble because it's this circle of grief. Like a shield to the outside world. One wrong move, one sympathy sentence away from being popped. You're just floating around with all these emotions.

Grief is lonely. Even though everyone grieves, no one grieves the same way you do. So, what you're feeling, the way you're surviving without your loved one, no one is surviving the same way you are.

And that's why grief is lonely.

WHEN

DOES

THE

PAIN

STOP

POETRY

Is just songs

In

slow motion..

GOD, Me and You

I remember those nights
in the hospital

just the three of us
as I would talk to you
I held one hand and apparently
he held one too
Just the three of us in the middle
of the night

God, me and you

I would stand there and tell you
how I plan to take you home

I just didn't know
that he was telling you that too
just the three of us

God, me and you

I SIMPLY

WRITE

MY

EMOTIONS

IT'S UP TO YOU

TO

REACT

you went ahead of me

when I get to

heaven

you can give

back

the pieces

of

my heart

as long as I breathe
I will miss you
As long as I miss
you

I will hurt
As long as I hurt
I will love you

DON'T FOCUS ONLY ON THAT GRIEF

THAT BRINGS YOU PAIN

AND

TOTALLY FORGET ABOUT EVERYTHING

THAT BRINGS YOU JOY

Don't be hard on yourself. If you're having a bad day, it's okay. That's what grief can be like.

A 1000 moments
I had taken for granted
only because I had
assumed
there would be at least

1000
more

*I wake up every day
and I realize
you're really gone*

You

You may not be here physically anymore

but in my heart

You will always be here

grief is love
Just
Stored in the
Heart

Sooner or later

I'm going to have
to think about it

And

I'm

going

To be

a mess

No matter how long the night

Morning is coming....

Maybe I'm just afraid
if I stop talking about
it

I'll stop hurting
If I stop hurting
I'm afraid I'll forget
Grief hurts, grief is
painful, grief sucks

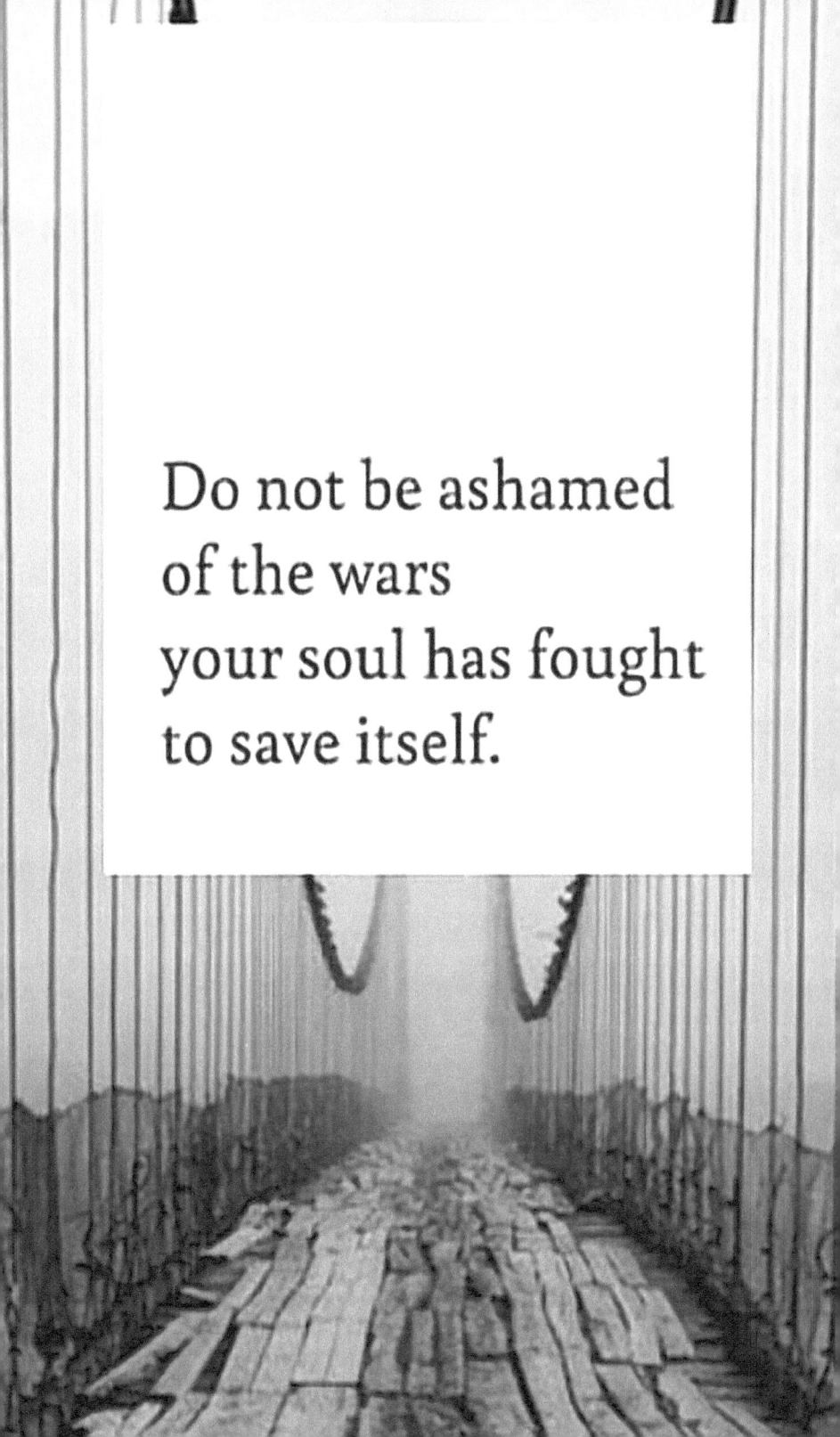

Do not be ashamed
of the wars
your soul has fought
to save itself.

Chapter Eleven

THOSE MOMENTS IN TIME

A 'moment in time' is **a particular time that something happens**.
A 'moment' usually refers to a noticeably brief period of time.

Grief is not the end, but it is hard. It is the beginning of major change in your life

whether you want it or not.

MOMENTS of LIFE

I mean we all know we have limited time here

But life has a way of distracting us with dreams,careers, weedy gardens and conversations.
While we're planning vacations and family get togethers. Life is slowly sneaking by
Or maybe
Those precious moments are Life...

what hurts the most
is that my world
felt like
it stopped turning

but the rest of the world turned on...

Life is full of moments that matter—moments of clarity, truth, love, and connection.

Moments that signify turning points, missed opportunities, fate, and luck.

We must face the reality that it's too late for us to change the past, and it does us no good to dwell aimlessly on things we wish we had said or done.

All of us have moments we shared with our loved ones who have died.

What we can do is look back on our relationships in the same way we would flip back through an enjoyable book.

Slowly soaking in all our favorite parts and feeling compassionate towards our actions, knowing that, when they happened, we did not have the benefit of hindsight.

As hard as it is to sit and think about those moments, those memories, they will become the very thing that gets you through this.

You will learn to cherish those thoughts and hold on to those memories. Looking back and searching your mind for special moments will be the comfort that heals and sustains you.

Don't be afraid to go there....

And this is why I say grief is not our enemy.

The absolute truth is the only thing
worse than losing our loved one
is the fear that they will be simply
forgotten.

I will never forget you...

Make your moments last

A

Life time

When you finally are able to slow the crying you can begin to move forward.

I feel sad
too
when I'm
without you

Can't just walk away

I guess I've come to far with grief to just
turn and walk away
I can't just pretend I'm ever going to be
the same
We met one early morning when I
received the pain
Oh I've come to far to just turn and
walk away
Grief has been my enemy, an enemy I've
asked to stay
I don't know how we got here, me and
grief today
There must be some higher reason or
else I'm just insane
Grief came at me brutal, grief came at
me with pain
And now I've learned with
or without him
I've no hope to be the same

Letting go of all the pain is so very important in any hope for a grief recovery.

It's very hard to let go of what was your normal, what was your world.

Concentrate on letting go of the fear, guilt, bitterness, anger and regrets.

Focus your energy on the love, joy, positive thoughts and happy memories.

grief.

Chapter Twelve

WE SIMPLY HATE GRIEF

But the truth is maybe we shouldn't?

Grief, as hard as it is, has a purpose, and it's actually a good one.

Once we lose someone close to us, grief steps in and what feels like an attack is the start of the healing process. You see, at that very moment, there is no possible way our mind can comprehend being without them. We are overwhelmed with sorrow, sadness, and hopelessness. Grief begins to numb our thoughts and feelings. Suddenly, appointments and schedules just don't matter as much and are not quite as important anymore.

Although it hurts immensely to think about our loss, that's exactly what we do, and grief gives us the tunnel vision to focus on almost nothing else. The world will keep right on turning, but for a brief period of time, maybe days, weeks or for some months, we just don't notice, and we simply don't care.

Grief, as hard and ruthless as it is, is actually allowing us some mental down time to adjust to the new reality.

As the time slowly creeps by, grief will begin to loosen its choking grip around you. Reality will begin to take over, and you find you have no choice but to be aware of your surroundings. You probably need to go back to work or possibly start to see friends and family again, and step by step you will move forward just by waking up each morning and pushing yourself out of bed.

This is when grief steps in for round two...

Now that you're trying to focus on your work, your kids, or maybe just yourself, you are feeling a little better knowing that you simply can't change any of this. Just as you're getting your thoughts back and making some measurable progress, you are going to wake up one morning, or maybe you will be driving down the road, and it's going to hit you.

This overwhelming realization that you and the world have moved forward, and the mere thought that you have joined the process and possibly forgot your loss and your loved one is going to break you with sadness.

You see, the thought of our loved one being forgotten is as bad as losing them.

This is where round two of grief's work begins.

Going on without your loved one, and somehow suppressing the feelings, is a feeling of betrayal that hurts so deep, so hard, that you will feel it's possibly worse than the actual loss.

Grief is not about to let that happen.

From the first look, that seems like punishment but once you experience that feeling of forgetting the person, forgetting the loss, once you taste that pain even for just a second, you will welcome the visit of grief. You may just be as I am where I say I would rather feel the pain and hurt than ever live without them.

Yes, this sounds like three steps forward and one step back, but healing can sometimes be slow. Sometimes we don't want to stop hurting all the way; sometimes the hurt is the reminder that we love them, and we need them.

Grief is just going to keep showing up and poking until you finally heal enough to deal with all the feelings and accept loss. They are always with you, and your love isn't measured by how much you hurt.

Chapter Thirteen

PET GRIEF

People often write to me on social media, and they ask, *what do you think about losing a pet?* And *do you think that it is grief we feel?*

There's only one answer. Absolutely yes.

Grief is grief, and it comes from the act of grieving. We grieve for many reasons, not just the death of a loved one but of our beloved pet and even the end of friendships and marriages.

I do not believe in ranking grief on some kind of a scale where one is ranked harder or considered worse than another. The pain and sorrow you feel from your loss whatever the circumstance is just as hard as the loss from any circumstance I might be having.

Losing a pet is a deep, life-changing event that can leave you with grief of the deepest portion. You can and will experience many of the exact feelings and emotions as you will when you suffer a loss of any other nature.

Animals offer us such loving companionship, emotional support, unconditional love, and endless joy. For many, their pet is a prominent part of the family. And our attachment to one another can sometimes be stronger than to other family members. So how could you not feel sorrow and pain from the loss of such love? It's only natural to grieve the loss of such attachment.

Yes, pet grief is just as real, and don't let anyone try and convince you otherwise. Finding ways to cope with the sorrow and emptiness is extremely important as you process and move forward on your healing journey.

Reaching out to others such as family and friends, support groups, and even their veterinarian are all excellent ideas to find companionship and resources during this time.

Taking the time to grieve and process the emotions is paramount and necessary to reach a point where you can feel joy and happiness from the memories and love that you shared with this special family member.

Chapter Fourteen

PERSONAL WRITINGS

Hello loneliness
my old friend

I see you've started staying
all night again
I often thought our relationship
would end
But you're so easy to talk to
as if you know me from within
I know I will regret this letting
you back in
Even though I will be left
hurting and sorry again
Sit here for just a moment
 I'm that desperate for a friend...

you went ahead of me

when I get to heaven

you can give back

the pieces of

 my heart

the crowd
 says
you have to recover
from grief

RECOVER ....

you don't recover from love
you hold on to it no matter
the pain...

Me

I don't recognize me in the
mirror anymore
The emptiness, the sadness
that hovers over me
Imprisoned for not a crime
that I did
but was laid upon me
Sentenced and shackled
against my will
Forever to carry the burden
and marks
of mental anguish
But if this is my only way
to feel
then cuff and chain me
for eternity

Grief

IS

THE

TROPHY

Of

LOVE

Forward

Is the only way

There simply is no

Going back

I write to keep from
crying
I cry to keep from
screaming
I scream to keep from
hurting
I hurt...
because
         you're
                  gone

I just can't seem to stop

starting all over again

We wrote our

story

And no one

Can take that

away from us

Do you see loneliness or hope?

Chapter Fifteen

IT'S OKAY TO NOT BE OKAY

Yes, I said it.

It's okay to not be okay. You don't have to meet or live up to anyone's expectations. You should and need to do what it takes to recover from this and that may not be what every friend and family member recommends.

People will come from everywhere with all their "supposably" good meaning remarks, but you will simply hear the stupidness in everything they say.

"Just pull yourself together."

"Lock these feelings away."

"Heaven needed them more than you."

"You will meet somebody else."

"You can get another pet"

Please, can I just give a little advice here? Say nothing. You really don't have to say anything to someone who just lost their loved one.

Just give a hug, a smile, maybe a handshake, but please SAY NOTHING. Don't feel the need to say some useless statement.

We are all different, and we need very different things to help us when we face these kinds of life situations.

For some of you, alone time is what you crave. A chance to just let it all soak in and just breathe. Healing comes through your thoughts and your memories.

For others, they need to be with someone, maybe everyone. Just the thought of being alone is overwhelming, and they seek out those friends and family members to stay close and give comfort.

There is no right way, only your way. So don't allow others to make you feel that you should carry yourself in any certain way.

Here are some suggested steps to try and start to cope with grief and loss.

1. Acknowledge your pain.

2. Accept that grief can trigger many different and unexpected emotions.

3. Understand that your grieving process will be unique to you.

4. Seek out face-to-face support from people who care about you.

5. Support yourself emotionally by taking care of yourself physically.

6. Recognize the difference between grief and depression.

1. You are going to need to acknowledge your pain.

Say it out loud. Admit to yourself and everyone around you that you are hurting, suffering, and that you are doing the best you can.

Do not even think about faking it or putting on a happy smile. There is no need for that. You don't owe anyone anything. This is about you and your feelings, and maybe I'm the first one to acknowledge that. So there, now that we have that out in the open...

It's okay to admit you're hurting.

I want you to let it sink in.

Never just push the pain down inside you somewhere as if you are that strong or you just have it all together because it will need to be dealt with, and you don't want to do that later in all areas of your life.

Pain doesn't just go away, it grows.

2. Accept the fact that grief will trigger your emotions.

No matter what you do, if you care even a little about your loved one, your emotions will be triggered at the most random of times.

It may be something you see or hear that reminds you. Maybe it takes you back to that moment in time, and your emotions will just take you over.

Don't be afraid of this, and don't run from it. Let it happen and learn to cherish everything and anything that gives you a second of love and memories.

Of course, I understand you can't just stand there crying in the middle of work. All memories are not good ones, but those moments in time are all we really have to hold on to, so don't push them away.

Learn to embrace them. Learn to store them up for when you need one.

3. Understand that your grieving process will be unique to you.

Grief is not one size fits all, so don't expect, because you know someone who went through it, that you now know what's about to happen.

You are going to feel all of this from the inside. That's very different from watching it happen. You need to do what it takes to get you through it, regardless of what it took someone else.

4. Please seek out face-to-face support.

Yes, I said do what you need to do. Stay in bed if you need to. Cry when you want to, and don't fake being fine ever.

But you are going to need support. You are going to need someone, maybe a lot of "someones" if you have it, that you can rely on and lean on.

Perhaps you have a great friend, neighbor, a family member, or a counselor.

Reach out to them and let them in on what you really are feeling.

Find someone that you can say the hard and scary things to, because I'm not the only one who ever had absolutely terrible thoughts. And if that's true, then you are having them also, and they need to come out. They need to be said and dealt with.

If you don't, they will grab you by the throat and choke you.
Reach out for help.

It can be through a local church, a grief support group, a helpline, or maybe a licensed counselor.

But take this seriously and reach for help.
The only shame is in suffering alone.

5. Help your emotional healing by supporting yourself physically.

If you have been working out, don't stop now. You need it more than ever. If you haven't been doing anything for your physical health, let this be a good time to start. Maybe just as simple as a walk each day.

Some time alone to just walk and clear your thoughts could be perfect for your mind and body.
Sadness affects the mind and body.

6. And finally, recognize the difference between grief and depression.

The similarities of these two are frighteningly close.

Grief is ever so overwhelming, and it has the ability to shut you down and numb your emotions.

You may seem hopeless at times and just can't see yourself making it through this. We may say words like "hopeless" and "devastated," but deep down, we truly know that we are going to find the way, the path to recover.

We know that we have people to reach out to. We have prayer to go to. Help if we only ask. Along with a will to survive anything that comes at us.

We know that, in time, we will get through this. Life will look different going forward, but we can and will adjust to it.

BUT FOR ANY REASON

If for any reason you don't feel that you can agree to any of that statement, you just can't truly believe that you are going to make it, I want you to immediately reach for help.

Call your friend, call your doctor, call a helpline, but take this seriously, and immediately reach out and confess your true feelings. Hold nothing back.

Hotlines that can help

- National Suicide Prevention Lifeline/National Crisis Hotline (800) 273-8255
- SAMHSA: Substance Abuse and Mental Health Services Administration (800) 662-4357
- Crisis Text Line - Text HOME to 741-741 in the U.S.
- LAP OF LOVE PET LOSS AND BEREAVEMENT RESOURCE LINE (855) 352-5683

It's
Okay
To

Not Be Okay

After you passed
weeks passed
months passed
but grief
he stayed
he's been here
day and night

Chapter Sixteen

THE TRUTH ABOUT GRIEF

You learn to go on

First you crumble and then you cry
You look around at your pieces on the
floor and you can't help but ask why

Your tears run like blood and you doubt
you will survive
But the earth continues to circle the sun
as day by day goes by

That's how you learn to go on

Little by little, bit by bit as you walk
around completely in a daze
You realize more and more you're not
there and they're not here,
 the sun goes up the sun goes down
and you don't even care

You spend your time in thoughts and
memories until people say they worry
for you, but what else can you do...

HOW LONG DOES GRIEF TAKE?

If I said a lifetime, would you close
this book and never return.
Because that just might be the
right answer. The truth is that there
is no right answer, it's different for
every person. We all deal with things
differently and heal at a different pace.
The main thing to take away here is
that you can heal, you will get better, as
long as you accept what's happened and
attempt to push forward.

That's how you learn to go on

It just doesn't feel right but you know it's
not wrong, to realize you just have to go
on
Just little by little you let the pain go
You learn there's other ways to keep
their love near

That's how you learn to go on

You lean into the storm and slowly
accept,
they live in your heart and they're never
really gone

 It's just up to you to carry on

Talk about your grief

The path to healing starts with talking about it. Most of our society silently says, "You deal with it on your own," but that's just not the right path for starting the healing process with grief.

Words like death, grief, died are just not common enough but if you want to get better and not carry this around your neck for years into the future. I say break the silence and talk.

Share your feelings, the good and the bad. You don't ever have to fake your feelings and paint a pretty picture. Just being real will help you to accept what has happened and start the journey to living with grief and not being controlled by it.

Be open, be honest, talk about it.

Loss changes us

It's true you just can't be the same you after experiencing a major loss in your life. Whether

It's a beloved family pet or a loved one. A little something dies inside of us, sometimes a big something.

Grieving and loss are most likely going to show you what the important things in your life really are. You will find yourself more compassionate and empathetic towards other people. Your priorities may shift and those little moments in time become of most importance.

Yes, there will be scarring and trails of where the tears ran but you can and will heal you just have to be willing to push forward.

MY WORDS
©Jwilkinsonauthor

Lately I've been lonely

Have you ever been completely
surrounded with people but
completely alone
Perhaps the gravity of forever
is sinking in
Realizing I will never get to talk
 to you again is overwhelming me
Suddenly your leaving has began
 to resemble my life sentencing
Suddenly living looks a worse
 fate then passing
And yet I know I shouldn't think out
loud like this

© jwilkinsonauthor

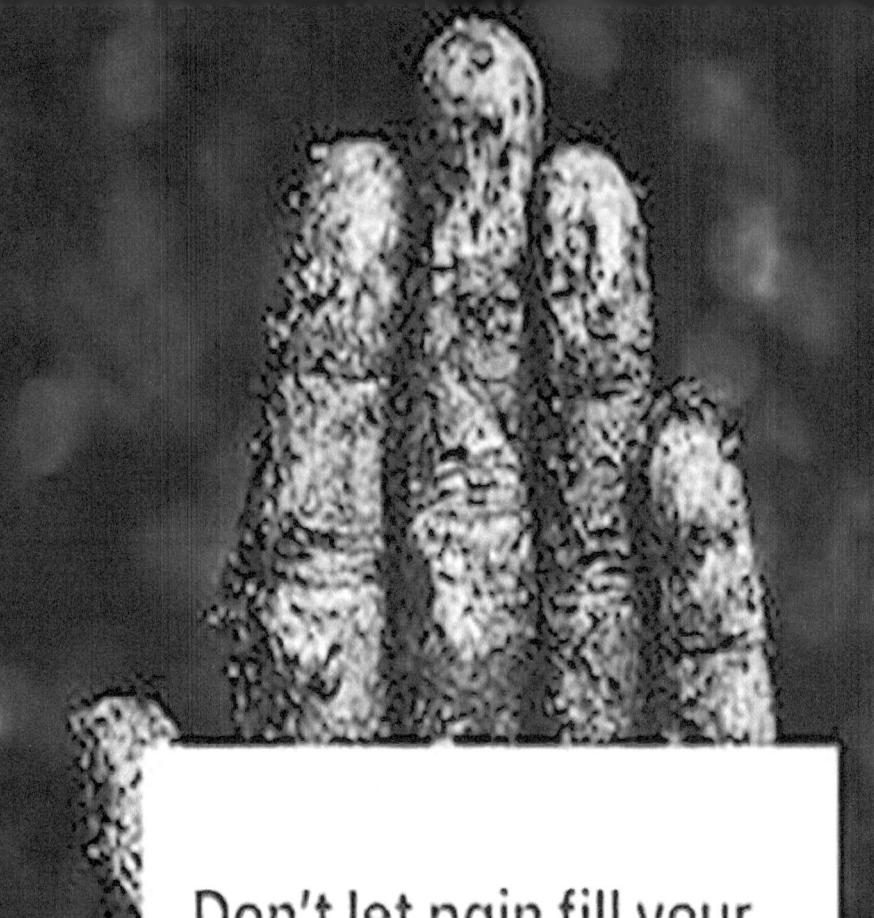

Don't let pain fill your
void
that place is reserved
for
memories and love

Don't do this alone

Grieving by nature is a very isolating journey.

You often feel no one really cares to hear you anymore and perhaps you feel no one really

even cares at all. The more you pull back the louder that voice gets. That's exactly why I say don't do this alone.

You need to reach out for help, you absolutely must do this. This could be a very trusted friend

or a local pastor. Join a grief group, possibly

seek out a counselor or specialist.

This is not the time to go it alone. I want to encourage you to take my advice and reach.

for help.

There's a struggle living inside of me

A rage about how things are and how they
use to be
I have to learn to live with this new me

There's a struggle living inside of me
How to go on
How do I adjust you see

There's a struggle living inside of me
Sometimes I wake in the middle of night and
it's right there choking me

There's a struggle living inside of me

Chapter Seventeen

MY THEORY

Throughout this book, we have talked and explored grief, sadness, and loss. We covered the five main stages of grief and lightly discussed how each one can surface in your day-to-day life. We talked about your need to reach out for help and how important it is to have someone you can share with; you simply are not a strong enough adversary to stand against grief all alone. Reaching out to a pastor, counselor, or support group would be highly recommended.

Grief is an extremely fierce enemy.

Grief has many weapons, sadness, loneliness, regret, hopelessness. It even has the ability to affect you physically. How are you going to stand up against that?

That's where my theory comes in.

While facing something that strong, that overpowering, perhaps we are looking at this all wrong. No one comes forward and states that they defeated grief. No one proclaims that they have been able to bottle grief up and just simply throw it out with the trash that day.

Absolutely no one can tell you how to just turn it off and place it on a shelf for a later day.

Why is that?

Why does grief get to slip under the closed door? Why does grief linger in the back of your thoughts just waiting for an opportunity?

Why with all the books written and all the attention that grief gets has no one ever mastered this emotion?

We all face it at some point in our lives. Absolutely no one is immune from being affected during their life, either directly or through acquaintances. Yet no real discovery has ever been made to stop the pain and sorrow that grief hands out. No one person has ever been able to say they have found the switch to turn off these overbearing feelings completely, never to return upon us again.

There simply must be some rational explanation for this.

Why, while eating lunch with my friend John (who is in his early 80s and his father has been gone for over 20 years), did he break down sobbing as he talked about his father and their relationship and life together.

Why did my good friend Jamie start to cry and quiver in his voice as I asked him questions about his father who had passed, and he began to tell me of his love for him and his family.

I think I may know the answer.

As I prepared for this book, through living my own journey of loss, through opportunities to speak with others at support groups, and the hundreds and possibly thousands of people I have had contact with through my previous book and my social media accounts—one thing has always stood out.

As mean and ugly as we say grief is, and believe me it does live up to its description, one thing constantly glared out at me.

The fear of our loved one being forgotten

You see, when we initially lose a loved one, we are all overwhelmed with the thought of not having contact with them in a physical sense. We can only focus on how we continue to live our lives and not have them here to experience it with us.

Just the thought of a normal daily routine is hard enough but add to that holidays and special events, and it all just becomes more than most can handle.

Just as you start to adjust mentally to the fact things are forever different, a new even bigger thought will consume you.

Are they being forgotten?

More people talk to me about this subject than death.

Perhaps it's because it feels like we're losing them again when we see the world just keeps on turning.

I closed my company for two days after my son passed, just because I needed to make everyone STOP, and it was all I had control over.

People have expressed to me how angry they felt walking into a grocery store and everyone was just going about their business as if this person's world hadn't just stopped.

Forgotten

Could anything really be worse?

We build mausoleums, giant monuments, and headstones to honor our loved ones. Of course, they don't even know this in most cases, so really, we do it for us, the surviving loved ones.

We do it to honor them and to mark their existence, to assure that not only we but everyone else will forever remember them.

What if grief subconsciously is doing the same?

What if grief is privately battling to make sure we never, ever are allowed to forget them? I am not saying we want to, but saying as time goes by and our lives go back to being busy, there are moments we forget the pain of loss. And let's be honest, we can't, in anyone's view, be expected to stay in a constant form of misery and loss. No one would even begin to think that was wise or rational.

Grief returns, with all its constantly ill-timed reminders and those overwhelming thoughts.

It comes in the blatantly loud signals and then the ever so tender nudges, like with my friend John who I assume had thought he was way past crying and sobbing at the mere mention of his beloved father.

Is it possible that grief is working with us?

Perhaps one could go as far as to say, "for us?"

Yes, my theory is that grief is not our enemy!

Even though it may feel like it most of the time, grief has a purpose. A purpose so big that we couldn't even move forward without it.

We must accept that grief will never let our loved one go, and through that power of forced remembrance, we will never completely lose our loved ones.

Grief can't bring them back, but grief can make sure the second biggest fear will never happen.

Grief can assure us they will not be forgotten, ever.

Grief makes sure they are always with us, inside us. And every so often, grief will fully remind us to stop and embrace those moments in time.

Chapter Eighteen

HOW DO WE SURVIVE GRIEF?

We accept grief for what it is and for what it does. No longer do we fight back at every uncomfortable moment. Understanding that fighting grief is just fighting ourselves. We need to accept that grief is going to be with us for a long time, perhaps the rest of our lives.

This journey is hard, and learning to carry your loved one inside you is difficult. But the alternative is worse.

NO, GRIEF IS NOT OUR ENEMY

Although grief feels like a negative opponent, and we curse grief for all that it puts us through, the real reason no one has ever been able to bottle it up or find the switch to turn it off is that grief is simply our own love for that lost loved one. It's working day and night to make sure we never allow ourselves or this world to forget just how much they meant to us and just how much the world lost with their passing.

So, my theory is that grief is not our enemy but simply our love working for us.

Moments in time

Don't run from those memories, run to them.

Those thoughts and moments in time that you often

remember are your lifeline to the past.

The past that you need and will be the very thing

that carries you through this journey we call grief.

Life is chronicled by the moment.

Whether looking forward or looking back, take the time to embrace those precious

Moments in Time.

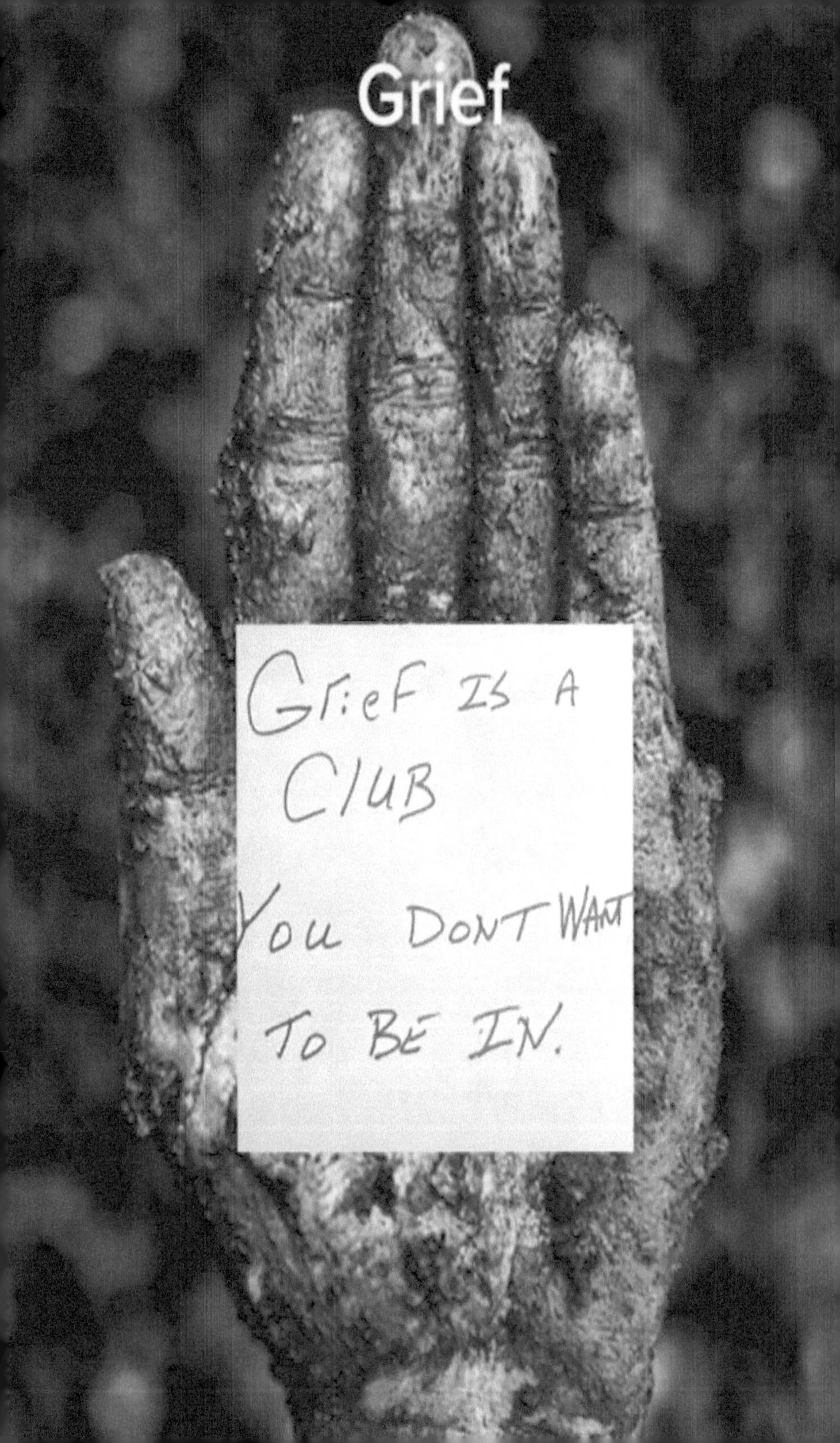
Grief
GRIEF IS A
CLUB
YOU DONT WANT
TO BE IN.

Helping others to heal

I really want to encourage you to consider volunteering

 to help others. There are so many ways to be of help to someone else and help meet their needs.

I think I know what you're thinking, you need help right now and you're in no place to help someone else. I can understand that thought but you are actually wrong on this one.

Helping someone else will get you out of your norm and give you a new perspective of what others are going through. You will get the satisfaction of knowing that you have a purpose and are still capable of contributing and it will offer you opportunities to share your unique story.

Don't go through something as life changing as this and not be willing to help someone.

You may be the very one to make the difference in someone else's journey and therefore help them to

 make it through.

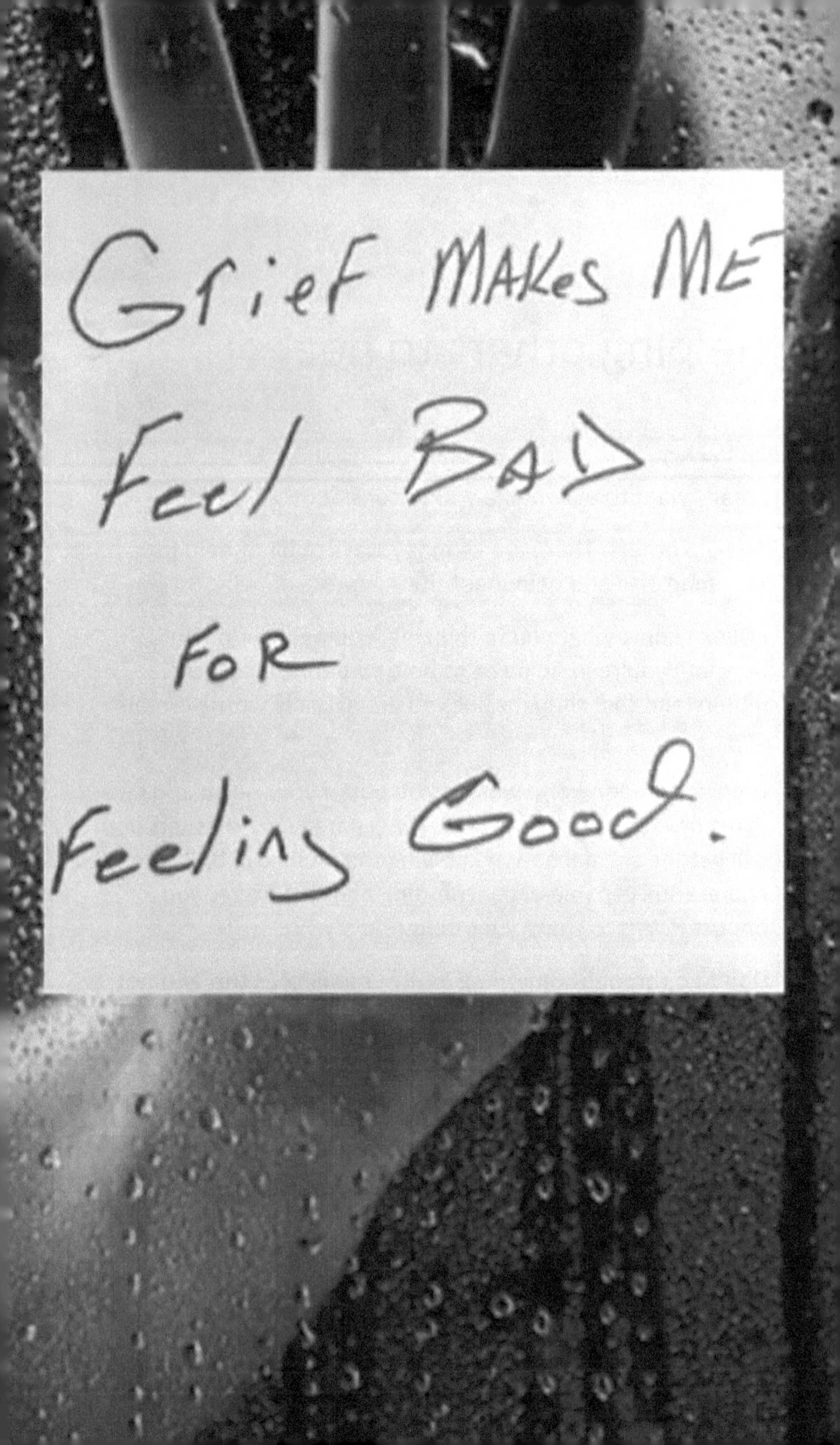
Grief Makes Me
Feel Bad
For
Feeling Good.

This heart

This heart has been broken this heart
has been used
This heart feels loss this heart
misses you
This heart has its locks this heart
has its cell
This heart is filled with grief
This heart has been through hell
This heart cried endlessly this heart
stayed true
This heart still knows love this heart still
loves you

Some form of grief may be with me for the rest of my life, but that doesn't mean I'm going to let it have control over me.

We have a lot of living still to do and being overwhelmed and miserable will not change any part of this situation.

We never forget but we can love.

We never leave them behind but we can move forward.

Grief

Yes
I said I'm okay
that doesn't mean it's all over

It just means
I'm okay
for the moment

Jwilkinsonauthor

Is it possible to love again? YES

Is it possible to be happy? YES

Your grief came from love, grief is just a mirrored image of your love.

Grief is extremely hard, but grief has a purpose and that is to remind you of a love that was so beautiful and so strong that you will never allow yourself to forget it.

Grief does not set the rules and you are more than capable of continuing

to love your loved one that passed and opening yourself to new love.

ABOUT THE AUTHOR

It's so hard for me to use the word "Author". You see I'm just a person who began to write several years ago to empty my mind, and free my thoughts. I'm just a normal guy who can't seem to turn it off. I'm also a father who lost his oldest son, so I just felt the need to write.

Thank you for reading this book.

I hope you connected with it, and it helps you on your journey.

I encourage you to consider my first book,

"Thoughts Poems and Dreams" and you can view more of my work and follow me on social media on:

TikTok, Instagram

@Jwilkinsonauthor.

Feel free to write me JWilkinsonauthor@gmail.com